OFFICIAL SQA MODEL PAPERS AND PAST PAPERS WITH SQA ANSWERS

Standard Grade General
MATHEMATICS

**Three Model Papers and
2001 to 2002 Past Papers**

First exam paper published in 1998.

Published by
Leckie & Leckie Ltd, 8 Whitehill Terrace, St. Andrews, Scotland KY16 8RN
tel: 01334 475656 fax: 01334 477392
hq@leckieandleckie.co.uk www.leckieandleckie.co.uk

Leckie & Leckie Project Team: Simon Appleford; Bruce Ryan; Andrea Smith
Cover Design Assistance: Mike Middleton

ISBN 1-84372-058-2

A CIP Catalogue record for this book is available from the British Library.

Printed in Scotland by Inglis Allen on environmentally friendly paper. The paper is made from a mixture of sawmill waste, forest thinnings and wood from sustainable forests.

® Leckie & Leckie is a registered trademark.

Leckie & Leckie

Introduction

The best way to prepare for exams is to practise, again and again, all that you have learned over the past year. Attempt these questions and check your solutions against these *Official SQA Answers*. But give yourself a real chance and be honest! Make sure you work through each problem thoroughly, showing the step-by-step calculations that produce each answer. Doing this will help you gain not only a proper understanding of each topic but also the maximum marks possible from the examiners! Developing this working habit now will make it easier to do this in the exam!

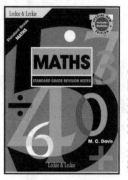

Standard Grade Maths Revision Notes. Whether you love numbers or realise that you just have to pass the exam, this is a crucial companion. Easy to refer to and full of relevant examples, this book is a winning formula!

ISBN 1-898890-77-3

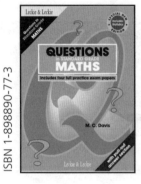

ISBN 1-898890-77-3

Questions in Standard Grade Maths. Probing problems on every aspect of the course that will help develop your mathematical abilities and confidence. Comes with two complete exam papers and a pull-out answer section.

Contents

FOR OFFICIAL USE

G

KU   RE

Total
marks

2500/403

NATIONAL
QUALIFICATIONS

Time: 35 minutes

BASED on the 1998 Question Paper

Due to the changes in format and syllabus
of the current paper, some amendments have
been made to the original paper.

MATHEMATICS
STANDARD GRADE
General Level
Paper 1
Non-calculator

Fill in these boxes and read what is printed below.

Full name of school or college

Town

First name and initials

Surname

Date of birth
Day Month Year   Candidate number   Number of seat

1 **You may not use a calculator**.

2 Answer as many questions as you can.

3 Write your working and answers in the spaces provided. Additional space is provided at
   the end of this question-answer book for use if required. If you use this space, write clearly
   the number of the question involved.

4 Full credit will be given only where the solution contains appropriate working.

5 Before leaving the examination room you must give this book to the invigilator. If you do
   not you may lose all the marks for this paper.

SCOTTISH
QUALIFICATIONS
AUTHORITY
©

FORMULAE LIST

Circumference of a circle:	$C = \pi d$
Area of a circle:	$A = \pi r^2$
Curved surface area of a cylinder:	$A = 2\pi rh$
Volume of a cylinder:	$V = \pi r^2 h$
Volume of a triangular prism:	$V = Ah$

Theorem of Pythagoras:

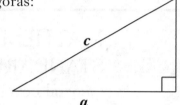

$$a^2 + b^2 = c^2$$

Trigonometric ratios
in a right angled
triangle:

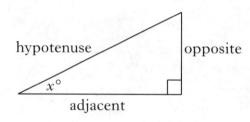

$$\tan x^\circ = \frac{\text{opposite}}{\text{adjacent}}$$

$$\sin x^\circ = \frac{\text{opposite}}{\text{hypotenuse}}$$

$$\cos x^\circ = \frac{\text{adjacent}}{\text{hypotenuse}}$$

Gradient:

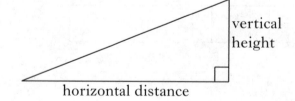

$$\text{Gradient} = \frac{\text{vertical height}}{\text{horizontal distance}}$$

	Marks	KU	RE

1. Carry out the following calculations:

(a) $1\cdot376 - 2\cdot93 + 3\cdot007$

1

(b) $39\cdot1 \div 5$

1

(c) 83×25

1

(d)   40% of 72 kilograms

2

DO NOT
WRITE IN
THIS
MARGIN

Marks

KU | RI

2. The temperature recorded at 6 am in Aviemore is shown on the diagram below.

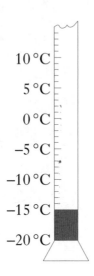

(a) By 9 am, the temperature had risen to −7 °C.

By how many degrees had the temperature risen?

1

(b) By 2 pm, the temperature had risen by a further 9 degrees.

What was the temperature at 2 pm?

1

DO NOT
WRITE IN
THIS
MARGIN

Marks

KU	RE

3. To raise money for its funds, a school organises a competition.

In this competition, each person selects **10** football teams.

Points are awarded as follows.

Points

Win	3
Score Draw	2
No-Score Draw	1
Loss	0

PRIZES ARE AWARDED
FOR **27 POINTS OR MORE**

One way of winning a prize is shown in the table below.

Number of teams getting 3 points	Number of teams getting 2 points	Number of teams getting 1 point	Number of teams getting 0 points	Total number of points
9	0	1	0	28

Complete the table to show all the different ways of winning a prize.

4

Marks

4. Michael's monthly salary is £720.

He spends $\frac{1}{5}$ of this on his mortgage, $\frac{3}{20}$ on his car and $\frac{1}{10}$ on insurance.

He uses the remainder for his household expenses.

(*a*) How much money does he spend on his car each month?

1

(*b*) What fraction of his monthly salary does he use for household expenses?

2

Marks

KU	RE

5. The amounts of money, in pence, spent by customers in a shop are shown below.

18	24	35	42	36	41	37	42	50	41	23	17
8	11	17	42	45	50	12	13	35	9	14	20

(a) Illustrate this data in an ordered stem and leaf diagram.

3

(b) What is the probability that a customer, chosen at random, spent more than 40 pence?

1

6. New York time is 5 hours behind British time.

When it is 7 pm in Britain, it is 2 pm in New York.

(*a*) At 10 am Gordon, who is in New York, phones home to Britain. What time is it in Britain?

1

(*b*) Los Angeles time is 3 hours behind New York time.

From Los Angeles, Fiona needs to phone a colleague in Aberdeen before 6 pm, British time.

She makes the phone call at 9.30 am, Los Angeles time.

Does she meet the 6 pm deadline?

Give a reason for your answer.

4

7.

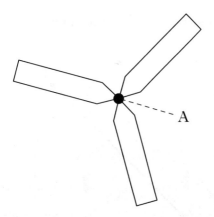

The logo above has rotational symmetry of **order 3** about point A.

Part of a company logo is shown below.

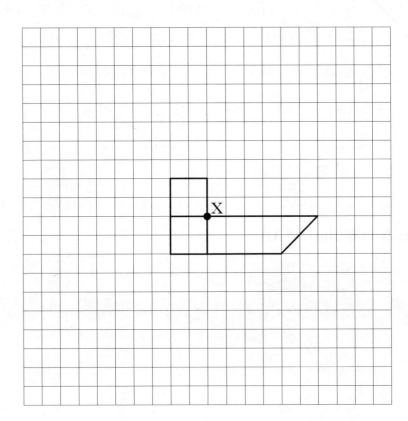

Complete the logo so that it has rotational symmetry of order 4 about point X.

3

Marks

KU | RE

8. The line AB is drawn on the coordinate diagram below.

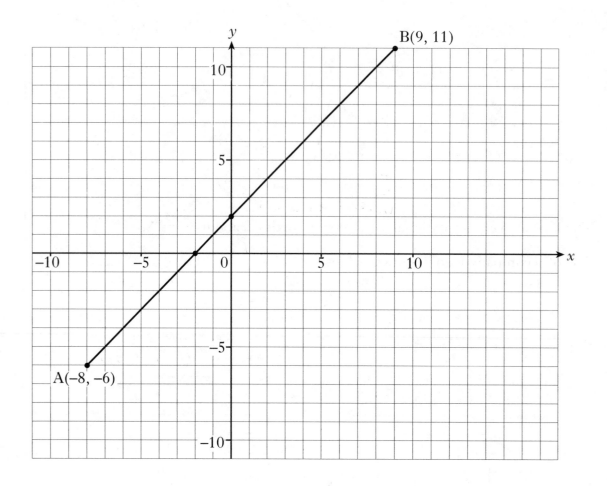

(*a*) Find the gradient of the line AB.

2

(*b*) On the same coordinate diagram, draw the line with equation $y = 2x - 4$.

2

Marks

DO NOT WRITE IN THIS MARGIN

KU	RE

9. (*a*) Tamara, Eva and Katrina are sisters.

Eva and Katrina are twins.

Tamara is 3 years older than the twins.

The total of the sisters' ages is 42 years.

Form an equation using the above information.

2

(*b*) Solve the equation to find Tamara's age.

2

[END OF QUESTION PAPER]

ADDITIONAL SPACE FOR ANSWERS

FOR OFFICIAL USE

G

	KU	RE
Total marks		

2500/404

NATIONAL
QUALIFICATIONS

Time: 55 minutes

BASED on the 1998 Question Paper

Due to the changes in format and syllabus of the current paper, some amendments have been made to the original paper.

MATHEMATICS
STANDARD GRADE
General Level
Paper 2

Fill in these boxes and read what is printed below.

Full name of school or college

Town

First name and initials

Surname

Date of birth
Day Month Year

Candidate number

Number of seat

1 **You may use a calculator**.

2 Answer as many questions as you can.

3 Write your working and answers in the spaces provided. Additional space is provided at the end of this question-answer book for use if required. If you use this space, write clearly the number of the question involved.

4 Full credit will be given only where the solution contains appropriate working.

5 Before leaving the examination room you must give this book to the invigilator. If you do not you may lose all the marks for this paper.

SCOTTISH
QUALIFICATIONS
AUTHORITY

DO NOT
WRITE IN
THIS
MARGIN

Marks

KU | R

1. One video costs £13·50.

On Special Offer is a set of 8 videos costing £104.

1 VIDEO — £13·50

SPECIAL OFFER

8-VIDEO SET—£104

(a) How much is saved by buying the set?

2

(b) Express the saving as a percentage of the cost of 8 single videos.

2

Marks

2. (*a*) Solve **algebraically** the inequality

$$7y + 3 < 24.$$

2

(*b*) Factorise $15w + 6st$.

2

Marks

| KU | RE |

3. The sides of a bridge are constructed by joining sections.

The sections are made of steel girders.

   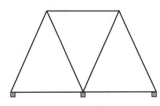   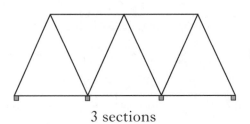

1 section
3 girders

2 sections
7 girders

3 sections

(*a*) Complete the table below.

Number of sections (*s*)	1	2	3	4		10
Number of girders (*g*)	3	7				

2

(*b*) Write down a formula for the number of girders, *g*, when you know the number of sections, *s*.

2

DO NOT
WRITE IN
THIS
MARGIN

KU | RE

3. (continued)

(c) Each section is an isosceles triangle.

The base is 11·25 metres long. The other girders are 15·65 metres long.

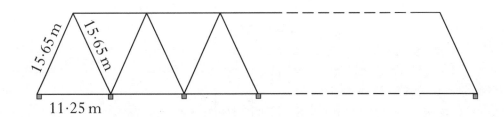

What is the total length of girders required for **one** side of a bridge 90 metres long?

4

Marks

KU | RI

4. The table below shows the distance in miles between different places in Scotland.

EDINBURGH

48	GLASGOW				
158	165	INVERNESS			
45	62	113	PERTH		
56	8	173	70	PAISLEY	
124	85	250	145	75	STRANRAER

(a) Use the table above to find the distance from Edinburgh to Paisley.

1

(b) Allan is a salesman whose office is in Edinburgh.

He gets travelling expenses at the rate of 27·5 pence per mile.

On Monday he travels from Edinburgh to Paisley and back.

How much does he get in travelling expenses?

2

(c) Each year, **after** he has travelled 8000 miles, Allan's expenses are reduced to 16·2 pence per mile.

In 1997, Allan travelled 9200 miles altogether.

What were his **total** travelling expenses for 1997?

3

DO NOT
WRITE IN
THIS
MARGIN

Marks

| KU | RE |

4. (continued)

(d)

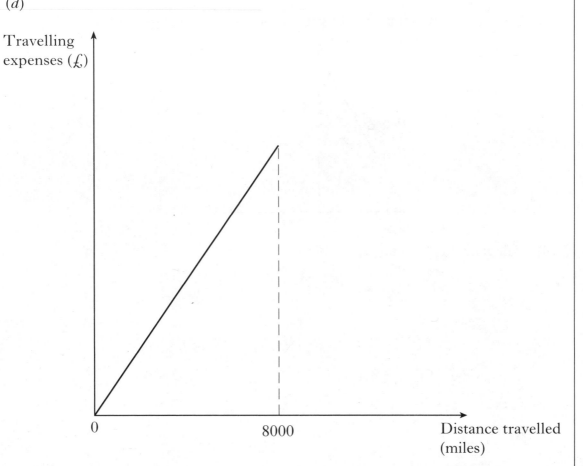

This graph shows, for part of 1997, the relationship between Allan's travelling expenses and the distance travelled.

Complete the graph for the remainder of 1997.   **2**

Marks

KU   R

5. A wall display cabinet is made in the shape of an equilateral triangle with length of side 40 centimetres.

One half of the cabinet has shelves; the other half has a glass door.

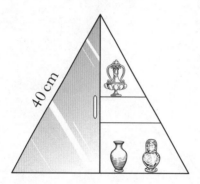

40 cm

(*a*) Calculate the height of the cabinet.

4

(*b*) Find the area of the glass door.

2

Marks

KU	RE

6.   A milk carton is in the shape of a cuboid with a square base.

The sides of the base are 8 centimetres long.

(a) The volume of the carton is 1280 cubic centimetres.

What is the height of the carton?

2

(b) A second cuboid carton, which also has a square base, holds 1·75 litres of milk.

The height of this carton is 25 cm.

Find the length of the base.

3

Marks

KU	RI

7. In the park, two new flower beds are being planted with roses.

8 m

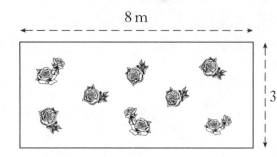

3·5 m

One flower bed is rectangular and measures 8 metres by 3·5 metres.

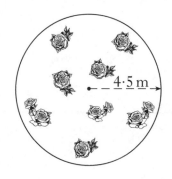

4·5 m

The other is circular with a radius of 4·5 metres.

(a) A fence is to be put around **each** flower bed.

Find the **total** length of fencing required.

3

(b) Fencing is sold by the metre.

What is the minimum length of fencing which must be bought?

1

DO NOT
WRITE IN
THIS
MARGIN

Marks

KU | RE

8.

54 mm

36 teeth

66 mm

The blade of a knife is
54 millimetres long.

The blade has 36 teeth.

The blade of a larger knife is
66 millimetres long.

The ratio   number of teeth   is the same for both knives.
            length of blade

How many teeth does the larger knife have?

2

DO NOT
WRITE IN
THIS
MARGIN

Marks

KU	RI

9. Superbuy Stores have a Friendly card which allows a shopper to collect points for money spent.

One point is given for each whole £1 spent.

(*a*) Anjum spends £27·26 in a Superbuy Store.

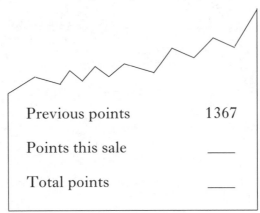

Previous points   1367

Points this sale   ____

Total points   ____

Complete his till receipt.   **2**

(*b*) When you buy petrol from Superbuy, you get 3 points for every £5 spent.

Points may be exchanged for goods.

How much must be spent on petrol to obtain a personal stereo worth 380 points?   **3**

Marks

KU	RE

10. The design of a trolley wheel is shown.

The manufacturer requires that **angle x must be more than 32°**.

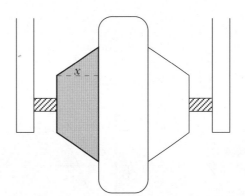

Part of this design has measurements as shown.

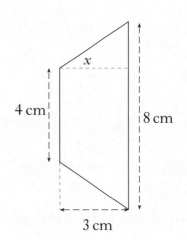

Do these measurements satisfy the manufacturer's requirements?

Give a reason for your answer.

Do not use a scale drawing.

4

DO NOT
WRITE IN
THIS
MARGIN

Marks

| KU | RI |

11.

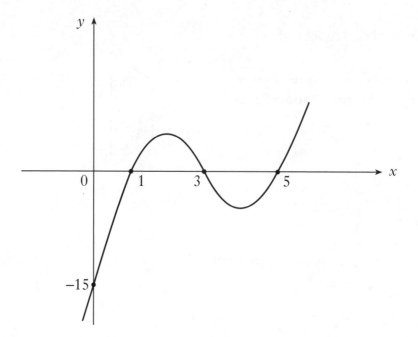

The diagram above shows the graph whose equation is $y = (x - 1)(x - 3)(x - 5)$.

Write down an equation for each of the graphs below.

(*a*)

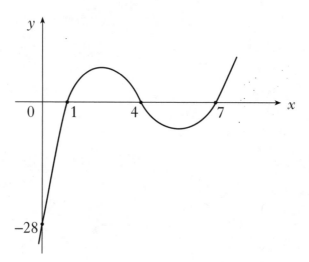

1

Marks

DO NOT
WRITE IN
THIS
MARGIN

KU   RE

11. (continued)

(b)

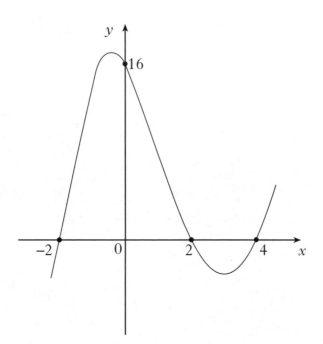

2

[END OF QUESTION PAPER]

ADDITIONAL SPACE FOR ANSWERS

G

FOR OFFICIAL USE

	KU	RE
Total marks		

2500/403

NATIONAL
QUALIFICATIONS

Time: 35 minutes

BASED on the 1999 Question Paper

Due to the changes in format and syllabus
of the current paper, some amendments have
been made to the original paper.

MATHEMATICS
STANDARD GRADE
General Level
Paper 1
Non-calculator

Fill in these boxes and read what is printed below.

Full name of school or college

Town

First name and initials

Surname

Date of birth
Day Month Year

Candidate number

Number of seat

1 **You may not use a calculator**.

2 Answer as many questions as you can.

3 Write your working and answers in the spaces provided. Additional space is provided at the end of this question-answer book for use if required. If you use this space, write clearly the number of the question involved.

4 Full credit will be given only where the solution contains appropriate working.

5 Before leaving the examination room you must give this book to the invigilator. If you do not you may lose all the marks for this paper.

SCOTTISH
QUALIFICATIONS
AUTHORITY

FORMULAE LIST

Circumference of a circle: $C = \pi d$
Area of a circle: $A = \pi r^2$
Curved surface area of a cylinder: $A = 2\pi rh$
Volume of a cylinder: $V = \pi r^2 h$
Volume of a triangular prism: $V = Ah$

Theorem of Pythagoras:

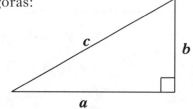

$$a^2 + b^2 = c^2$$

Trigonometric ratios
in a right angled
triangle:

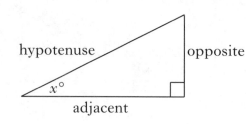

$$\tan x° = \frac{\text{opposite}}{\text{adjacent}}$$

$$\sin x° = \frac{\text{opposite}}{\text{hypotenuse}}$$

$$\cos x° = \frac{\text{adjacent}}{\text{hypotenuse}}$$

Gradient:

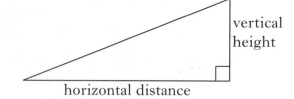

$$\text{Gradient} = \frac{\text{vertical height}}{\text{horizontal distance}}$$

DO NOT
WRITE IN
THIS
MARGIN

Marks

KU | RE

1. Carry out the following calculations.

   (a) $7 \cdot 8 - 3 \cdot 26 + 5 \cdot 75$

   1

   (b) $785 \div 500$

   1

   (c) $2 \cdot 39 \times 2000$

   1

   (d)   5% of £4·80

   2

Marks

KU	RE

2. The marks of a group of students in a practice test and in the final exam are shown in the scattergraph below.

A line of best fit has been shown.

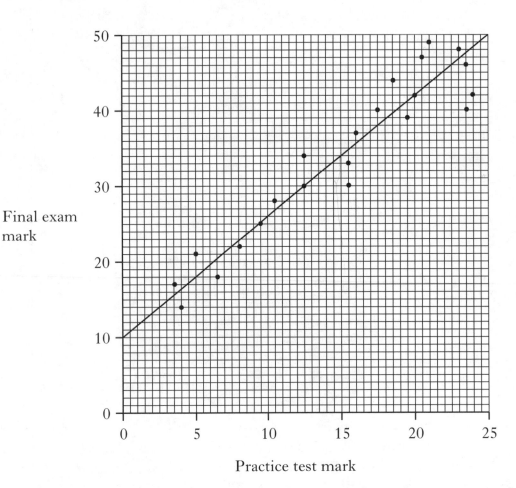

Final exam mark

Practice test mark

(a) What is the highest mark in the final exam?

1

(b) A student whose mark in the practice test was 15 did not attend the final exam.

Using the line of best fit, estimate this student's mark in the final exam.

1

Marks

KU	RE

3. (*a*) Draw the next T-shape in this sequence.

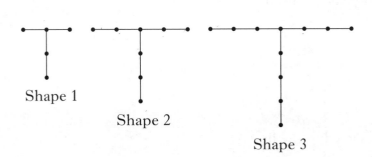

Shape 1

Shape 2

Shape 3

Shape 4   1

(*b*) Complete the following table.

Shape Number (s)	1	2	3	4	5		16
Number of dots (d)	5		11				

2

(*c*) Write down a formula for the number of dots (*d*) when you know the shape number (*s*).

2

(*d*) 101 dots are used in drawing a T-shape.

What is its shape number?

2

Marks

KU	RF

4. Ticketmasters Call Centre can handle 240 calls for concert tickets every 2 hours.

How many calls can they handle in 45 minutes?

2

5. The two shapes below are reflected in the line AB.

Draw the new positions of the two shapes.

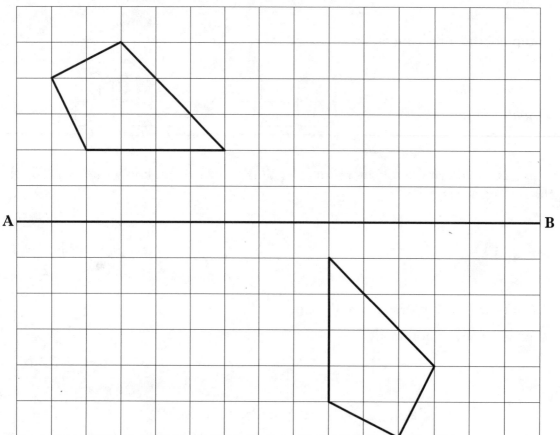

2

DO NOT
WRITE IN
THIS
MARGIN

Marks

| KU | RE |

6.   __Rule:__ **The number in the square is the sum of the numbers in the circles on either side of it.**

(−3)——[4]——(7)

(a) Use this rule to complete the diagram below.

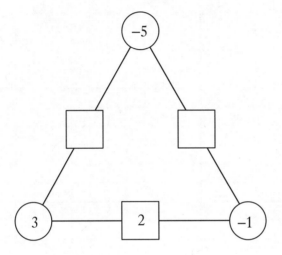

2

(b) Using the rule, enter the numbers −2, −1, 1, and 3 in the diagram below.

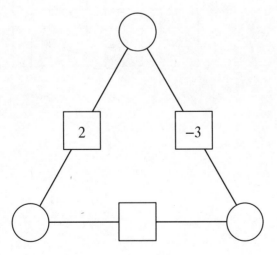

2

Marks

KU	R

7. *(a)*   Complete the table below for $y = 3x + 1$.

x	−3	0	3
y			

2

(b)   Using the table in part *(a)*, draw the graph of the line $y = 3x + 1$ on the grid below.

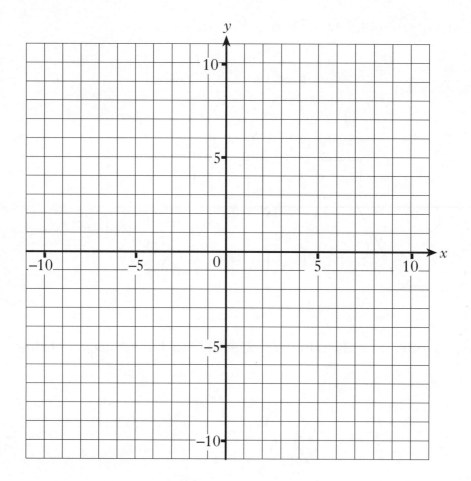

2

8.

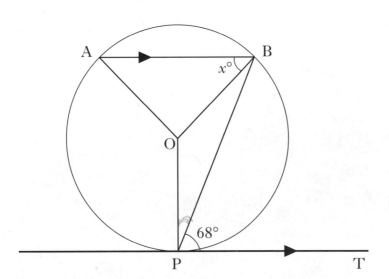

PT is a tangent to the circle, centre O.

PT is parallel to AB.

Angle BPT = 68°.

(*a*) What is the size of the angle BPO?

1

(*b*) Calculate the size of the angle marked *x*°.

3

Marks

KU | R

9. A sculpture is to be made by stacking three blocks of stone.

Each block of stone is a cube of side (1.2 ± 0.05) metres.

What is the maximum height of the sculpture?

2

[*END OF QUESTION PAPER*]

FOR OFFICIAL USE

G

Total marks

KU   RE

2500/404

NATIONAL
QUALIFICATIONS

TIME: 55 minutes

BASED on the 1999 Question Paper

Due to the changes in format and syllabus
of the current paper, some amendments have
been made to the original paper.

MATHEMATICS
STANDARD GRADE
General Level
Paper 2

Fill in these boxes and read what is printed below.

Full name of school or college

Town

First name and initials

Surname

Date of birth
Day Month Year   Candidate number   Number of seat

1 **You may use a calculator**.

2 Answer as many questions as you can.

3 Write your working and answers in the spaces provided. Additional space is provided at
   the end of this question-answer book for use if required. If you use this space, write clearly
   the number of the question involved.

4 Full credit will be given only where the solution contains appropriate working.

5 Before leaving the examination room you must give this book to the invigilator. If you do
   not you may lose all the marks for this paper.

SCOTTISH
QUALIFICATIONS
AUTHORITY

©

FORMULAE LIST

Circumference of a circle: $C = \pi d$
Area of a circle: $A = \pi r^2$
Curved surface area of a cylinder: $A = 2\pi rh$
Volume of a cylinder: $V = \pi r^2 h$
Volume of a triangular prism: $V = Ah$

Theorem of Pythagoras:

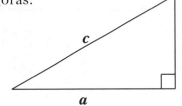

$$a^2 + b^2 = c^2$$

Trigonometric ratios
in a right angled
triangle:

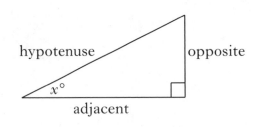

$$\tan x° = \frac{\text{opposite}}{\text{adjacent}}$$

$$\sin x° = \frac{\text{opposite}}{\text{hypotenuse}}$$

$$\cos x° = \frac{\text{adjacent}}{\text{hypotenuse}}$$

Gradient:

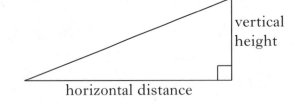

$$\text{Gradient} = \frac{\text{vertical height}}{\text{horizontal distance}}$$

DO NOT
WRITE IN
THIS
MARGIN

Marks

KU	RE

1. Mr and Mrs Donaldson are having a party to celebrate their 25th Wedding Anniversary.

   They want to buy Champagne.

   They see this sign in a shop window.

   CHAMPAGNE

   £24·99 per bottle

   15% Discount when you buy 6 bottles

   Calculate the cost of 6 bottles.

   3

Marks

DO NOT
WRITE IN
THIS
MARGIN

KU	RI

2. Two lenders, Mortgages Direct and Leading Mortgage, offer mortgages at different rates on a loan of £45 000.

Mortgages Direct	**Leading Mortgage**
Monthly payment £330·50	Monthly payment £349·90
Plus	And
One-off set-up fee £500	No other fees to pay

Which mortgage would be better value over a period of 3 years and by how much?

5

DO NOT
WRITE IN
THIS
MARGIN

Marks

KU | RE

3. A football pitch used in the Premier League measures 105 metres by 68 metres.

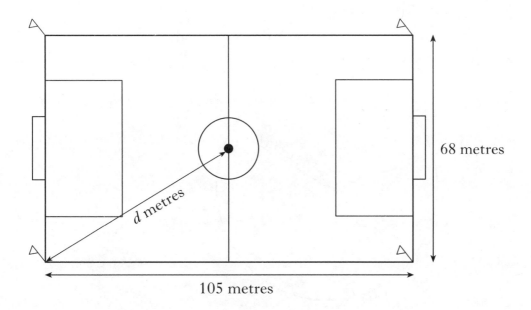

68 metres

d metres

105 metres

Find the distance, *d* metres, from the corner flag to the centre spot.

4

DO NOT
WRITE I
THIS
MARGIN

Marks

KU   R

4. A battery operated toy train travels on a circular track.

The radius of the circle is 40 centimetres.

It takes one minute for the train to travel 8 times round the track.

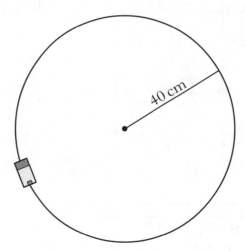

(*a*) How far does the train travel in one minute?

Give your answer to the nearest 10 centimetres.

4

(*b*) Find the speed of the train in centimetres per second.

2

Marks

KU	RE

5. The angle of elevation from the ground to the top of a block of flats is 48°.

The angle is measured at a point 75 metres from the flats as shown in the diagram below.

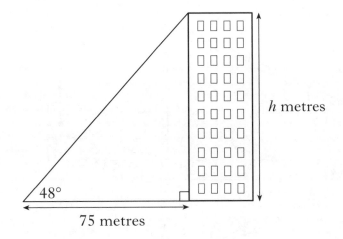

h metres

48°

75 metres

Calculate the height, *h* metres, of the block of flats, correct to 1 decimal place.

4

DO NOT
WRITE IN
THIS
MARGIN

Marks

KU | RI

6. Amy needs to replace fencing in her garden.

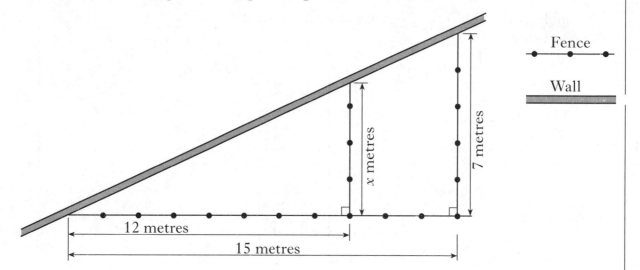

She has taken the measurements shown above, but has forgotten to measure the part of the fence marked *x* metres.

The garden centre has only 28 metres of fencing in stock.

Is this enough to completely replace the existing fencing?

4

DO NOT WRITE IN THIS MARGIN

Marks

KU	RE

7. (*a*)   Multiply out the brackets and simplify

$$2a + 3(4a - 5).$$

2

(*b*)   Solve **algebraically** the equation

$$4x - 3 = x + 5.$$

3

Marks

KU	R

8.

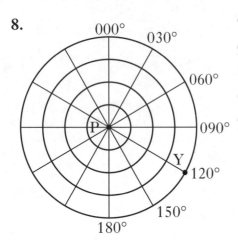

The diagram shows a Coastguard's radar screen.

The circles on the screen have radii of 10 km, 20 km, 30 km, and 40 km.

On the radar screen, port P is at the centre.

The yacht Y is also shown on the radar screen.

(a)   Plot the position of yacht Y on the map.

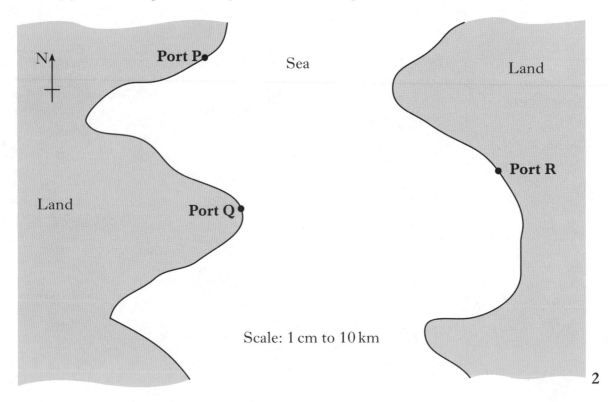

Scale: 1 cm to 10 km

2

Marks

KU	RE

8. (continued)

(b) The Coastguard receives a warning of bad weather and advises the yacht to sail to the nearest port.

To which port should the yacht sail?

Give a reason for your answer.

2

(c) Find the bearing and the distance from the yacht to the nearest port.

2

Marks

DO NOT
WRITE I
THIS
MARGIN

KU   R.

9. A pattern of circular discs of **diameter 6 centimetres** is to be cut from a
    square sheet of plastic.

    The diagram below shows part of this sheet.

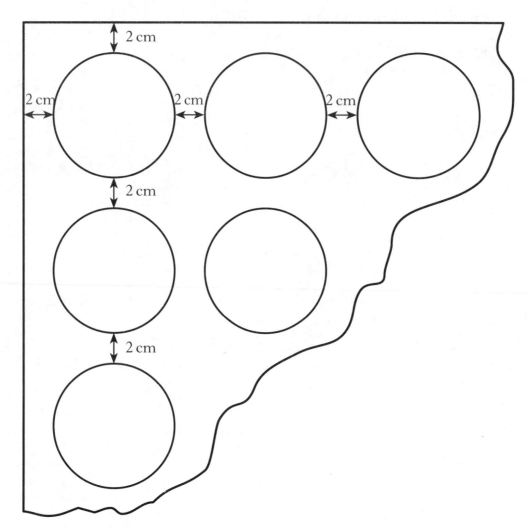

    (a) How many circular discs could be cut from a square sheet of plastic of
        side 50 centimetres?

        3

    (b) Find the area of plastic remaining after the discs have been cut from the
        square sheet.

        4

Marks

10. The distance to the horizon, *d* kilometres, varies as the square root of the height, *h* metres, above sea level.

The distance to the horizon is 14·4 kilometres at a height of 16 metres above sea level.

Calculate the distance to the horizon at a height of 25 metres above sea level.

4

DO NOT
WRITE IN
THIS
MARGIN

Marks

KU   RI

11.

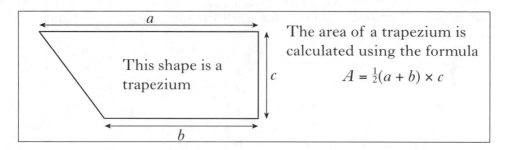

The area of a trapezium is calculated using the formula

$$A = \tfrac{1}{2}(a + b) \times c$$

This shape is a trapezium

The diagram below shows part of a rainwater gutter.

The ends of the gutter are identical.

Each end is in the shape of a trapezium.

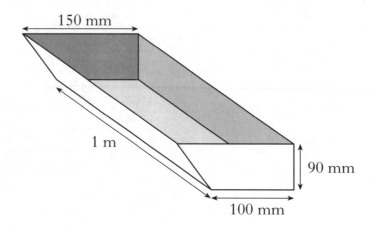

150 mm

1 m

90 mm

100 mm

Calculate the **volume** of this part of the gutter.

4

[END OF QUESTION PAPER]

FOR OFFICIAL USE

G

	KU	RE
Total marks		

2500/403

NATIONAL QUALIFICATIONS

Time: 35 minutes

BASED on the 2000 Question Paper

Due to the changes in format and syllabus of the current paper, some amendments have been made to the original paper.

MATHEMATICS
STANDARD GRADE
General Level
Paper 1
Non-calculator

Fill in these boxes and read what is printed below.

Full name of centre

Town

Forename(s)

Surname

Date of birth
Day Month Year   Scottish candidate number   Number of seat

1 **You may not use a calculator**.

2 Answer as many questions as you can.

3 Write your working and answers in the spaces provided. Additional space is provided at the end of this question-answer book for use if required. If you use this space, write clearly the number of the question involved.

4 Full credit will be given only where the solution contains appropriate working.

5 Before leaving the examination room you must give this book to the invigilator. If you do not you may lose all the marks for this paper.

SCOTTISH
QUALIFICATIONS
AUTHORITY

©

FORMULAE LIST

Circumference of a circle: $C = \pi d$
Area of a circle: $A = \pi r^2$
Curved surface area of a cylinder: $A = 2\pi rh$
Volume of a cylinder: $V = \pi r^2 h$
Volume of a triangular prism: $V = Ah$

Theorem of Pythagoras:

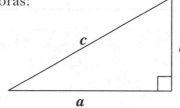

$$a^2 + b^2 = c^2$$

Trigonometric ratios
in a right angled
triangle:

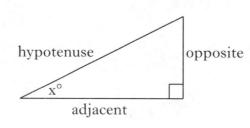

$$\tan x° = \frac{\text{opposite}}{\text{adjacent}}$$

$$\sin x° = \frac{\text{opposite}}{\text{hypotenuse}}$$

$$\cos x° = \frac{\text{adjacent}}{\text{hypotenuse}}$$

Gradient:

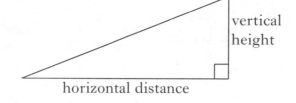

$$\text{Gradient} = \frac{\text{vertical height}}{\text{horizontal distance}}$$

1. Carry out the following calculations.

Marks

KU	RE

(a) $13 \cdot 3 + 25 \cdot 4 - 7 \cdot 52$

1

(b) $24 \cdot 92 \div 7$

1

(c) $5 \cdot 7 \times 400$

1

(d) $7 \times 2\frac{1}{3}$

2

Marks KU   RI

2. The distance from the earth to the sun is $1 \cdot 58 \times 10^{-5}$ light years.

Write this number in full.

2

3.

Here is part of a French Railway timetable for a high-speed train.

Distance from Paris (km)		
0	Paris	Depart 1644
512	Lyon	Depart 1900
617	Valence	Depart 1955
742	Avignon	Depart 2051
863	Marseille	Arrive 2144

(*a*) Calculate the journey time from Paris to Marseille.

1

(*b*) Find the speed of the train from Paris to Marseille.

Round your answer to the nearest kilometre per hour.

3

DO NOT
WRITE IN
THIS
MARGIN

Marks | KU | RE

4. To get money from a cash machine you need an appropriate card and a four digit Personal Identity Number (PIN).

David knows:

- his PIN contains the digits 2, 5, 6 and 9;
- 2 is the first digit.

One possible PIN is shown in the table below.

Complete the table to show all the possible PINs.

2	5	6	9

3

Marks | KU | RI

5. This table shows insurance premiums for holidays abroad.

INSURANCE PREMIUM per person				
	Europe		Rest of the World	
Duration of Holiday	Adult * (16–64)	Child (0–15)	Adult * (16–64)	Child (0–15)
Up to 8 days	£27·50	£19·50	£42·50	£37·50
9–16 days	£35·00	£30·00	£51·20	£47·00
17–24 days	£39·50	£35·00	£60·20	£56·00
* Premiums double for persons 65 years and over				

Mr and Mrs Jones, both 35 years old, take their two children, aged 3 and 8, and Mr Jones's father, aged 70, on a one week holiday to Europe.

Find the total cost of the insurance premium.

3

Marks | KU | RE

6. Draw the image of the shape reflected in the line AB.

4

Marks | KU | R

7. The operation ✦ means "square the first number and multiply by the second".

> For example, $5 ✦ 3 = 5^2 \times 3 = 25 \times 3 = 75$

(*a*) Evaluate $6 ✦ 4$.

1

(*b*) If $a ✦ 5 = 245$, find a.

2

Marks   KU   RE

8. The faces of a cube have the numbers 0, 1, 2, 3, 4 and 5 written on them.

Different views of this cube are shown in Diagrams 1 and 2.

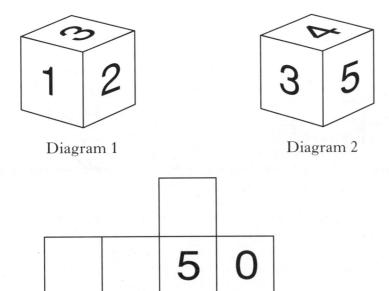

Diagram 1   Diagram 2

The net of this cube is shown above.

Fill in the remaining numbers on the correct faces.   **3**

Marks   KU   RI

9.   (a)   In a parking area there were 49 family cars, 15 sports cars and 11 four-wheel-drive vehicles. What is the probability that the first car leaving the parking area is a sports car?

1

    (b)   The first car that left was a sports car.

        What is the probability that the next car leaving the parking area is a family car?

2

Marks | KU | RE

10. In the diagram below PR is a diameter of the circle.

PS is a tangent to the circle at P.

Angle QPR = 48° and angle PSR = 33°.

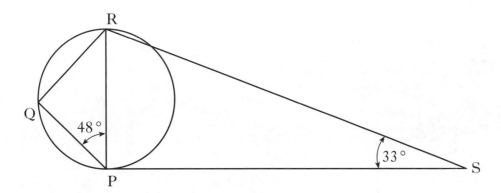

(*a*) Write down the size of angle PQR. Give a reason for your answer.

1

(*b*) **Calculate** the size of angle QRS.

3

[END OF QUESTION PAPER]

ADDITIONAL SPACE FOR ANSWERS

FOR OFFICIAL USE

G

	KU	RE
Total marks		

2500/404

NATIONAL   Time: 55 minutes
QUALIFICATIONS

BASED on the 2000 Question Paper

Due to the changes in format and syllabus
of the current paper, some amendments have
been made to the original paper.

MATHEMATICS
STANDARD GRADE
General Level
Paper 2

Fill in these boxes and read what is printed below.

Full name of centre

Town

Forename(s)

Surname

Date of birth
Day Month Year   Scottish candidate number   Number of seat

1 **You may use a calculator.**

2 Answer as many questions as you can.

3 Write your working and answers in the spaces provided. Additional space is provided at
   the end of this question-answer book for use if required. If you use this space, write clearly
   the number of the question involved.

4 Full credit will be given only where the solution contains appropriate working.

5 Before leaving the examination room you must give this book to the invigilator. If you do
   not you may lose all the marks for this paper.

SCOTTISH
QUALIFICATIONS
AUTHORITY

FORMULAE LIST

Circumference of a circle: $C = \pi d$
Area of a circle: $A = \pi r^2$
Curved surface area of a cylinder: $A = 2\pi rh$
Volume of a cylinder: $V = \pi r^2 h$
Volume of a triangular prism: $V = Ah$

Theorem of Pythagoras:

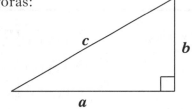

$$a^2 + b^2 = c^2$$

Trigonometric ratios
in a right angled
triangle:

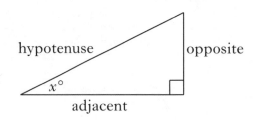

$$\tan x° = \frac{\text{opposite}}{\text{adjacent}}$$

$$\sin x° = \frac{\text{opposite}}{\text{hypotenuse}}$$

$$\cos x° = \frac{\text{adjacent}}{\text{hypotenuse}}$$

Gradient:

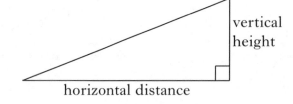

$$\text{Gradient} = \frac{\text{vertical height}}{\text{horizontal distance}}$$

Marks | KU | RE

1. The Computer Store buys this computer for £250 and sells it to make a profit of 40%.

(a) What is the selling price of this computer?

2

(b) The Computer Store adds 20% to the **selling price** when a customer buys the computer on hire purchase.

Hire purchase terms are a £30 deposit followed by 24 equal monthly payments.

Calculate the customer's monthly payment.

4

Marks | KU | R

2. A survey of the word lengths in a passage of 100 words was taken from a newspaper.

The results are shown in the table below.

Number of letters per word	Frequency	Number of letters per word × frequency
1	5	
2	12	
3	18	
4	26	
5	18	
6	11	
7	7	
8	3	
	Total = 100	

Complete the table above and find the **mean** length of a word.

3

Marks | KU | RE

3. A mountain railway tunnel is 800 metres long.

It rises 225 metres vertically.

Calculate the size of the angle marked $x°$.

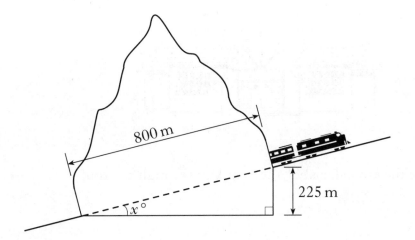

3

Marks   KU   R

4. A house loses heat through its roof, walls, windows and doors.

In the Grant family's bungalow 23% of its heat loss is through the roof.

The **total** heat loss from the house costs the Grant family £650 each year.

(a) Calculate the annual cost of the heat loss through the roof.

2

(b) If the Grant family insulate their loft, the heat lost through the roof will be reduced by two thirds.

How much money will they save each year if they insulate their loft?

2

(c) It will cost the Grants £750 to insulate their loft.

How long will it take them to recover their expenditure on the insulation?

2

Marks | KU | RE

5. Part of a straight line graph is shown below.

The line can be extended in either direction.

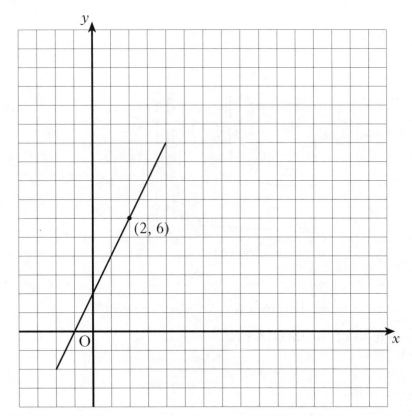

(a) Complete the table below to show the coordinates of some of the points on the straight line.

x	1	2	3	4	5	6
y		6				

2

(b) Write down a formula for finding y when you know x.

$$y =$$

2

(c) The point $(a, 22)$ lies on the straight line.

Find a.

2

Marks | KU | RE

6. The opening of the fireplace, shown in the diagram below, consists of a rectangle and a semi-circle.

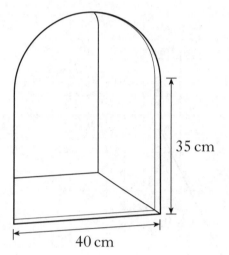

A metal strip is to be placed around the fireplace opening.

Calculate the length of the metal strip.

4

Marks | KU | RE

7. A sketch of a steel panel for a piece of machinery is shown below.

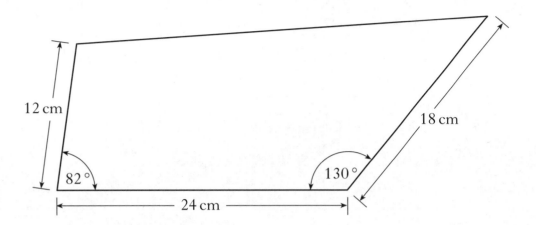

(*a*) Using a scale of 1:3, make a scale drawing of the steel panel.

3

(*b*) Use your scale drawing to find the **actual** length of the fourth side of the steel panel.

2

Marks   KU   RF

8. (*a*) Solve **algebraically** the equation

$$4x - 5 = x + 22.$$

2

(*b*) Factorise

$$8a - 12b.$$

2

Marks | KU | RE

9. This is part of a tiling of **congruent** kites.

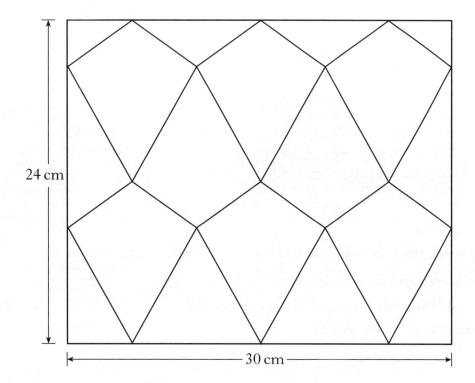

Calculate the area of one kite.

4

Marks | KU | RI

10. John is starting to lay concrete foundations for a garden wall.

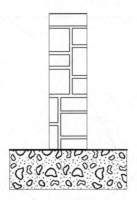

Concrete is made from stones, sand and cement, to which water is added.

He will mix stones and sand in the ratio 3 to 1.

(a) John needs 1·8 cubic metres of stones for the job.

How much sand will he need?

1

(b) One bag of sand has a volume of 0·075 cubic metres.

How many bags of sand should he buy for the job?

2

Marks

11. A new regulation states that the gradient of all ramps into a building must be less than 0·26.

An existing ramp is 410 cm long and has a horizontal distance of 400 cm.

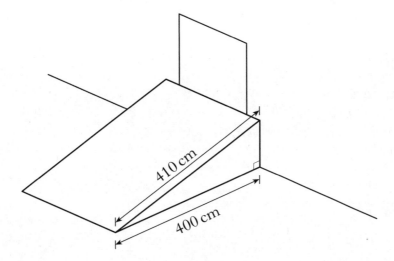

Does this ramp satisfy the new regulation?

Show all your working and give a reason for your answer.

5

[END OF QUESTION PAPER]

ADDITIONAL SPACE FOR ANSWERS

FOR OFFICIAL USE

G

Total marks	KU	RE

2500/403

NATIONAL
QUALIFICATIONS
2001

WEDNESDAY, 16 MAY
10.40 AM – 11.15 AM

MATHEMATICS
STANDARD GRADE
General Level
Paper 1
Non-calculator

Fill in these boxes and read what is printed below.

Full name of centre

Town

Forename(s)

Surname

Date of birth
Day Month Year

Scottish candidate number

Number of seat

1 **You may not use a calculator.**

2 Answer as many questions as you can.

3 Write your working and answers in the spaces provided. Additional space is provided at the end of this question-answer book for use if required. If you use this space, write clearly the number of the question involved.

4 Full credit will be given only where the solution contains appropriate working.

5 Before leaving the examination room you must give this book to the invigilator. If you do not you may lose all the marks for this paper.

SCOTTISH
QUALIFICATIONS
AUTHORITY

FORMULAE LIST

Circumference of a circle: $C = \pi d$
Area of a circle: $A = \pi r^2$
Curved surface area of a cylinder: $A = 2\pi rh$
Volume of a cylinder: $V = \pi r^2 h$
Volume of a triangular prism: $V = Ah$

Theorem of Pythagoras:

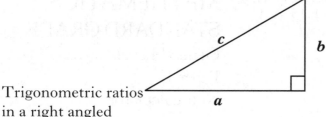

$$a^2 + b^2 = c^2$$

Trigonometric ratios
in a right angled
triangle:

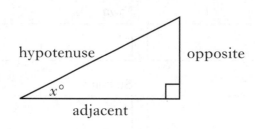

$$\tan x° = \frac{\text{opposite}}{\text{adjacent}}$$

$$\sin x° = \frac{\text{opposite}}{\text{hypotenuse}}$$

$$\cos x° = \frac{\text{adjacent}}{\text{hypotenuse}}$$

Gradient:

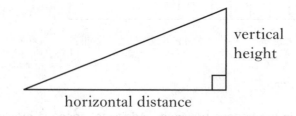

$$\text{Gradient} = \frac{\text{vertical height}}{\text{horizontal distance}}$$

DO NOT
WRITE IN
THIS
MARGIN

Marks	KU	RE

1. Work out the following.

(a) $18 \cdot 54 + 0 \cdot 61 - 5 \cdot 3$

1

(b) $3 \cdot 36 \times 70$

1

(c) $0 \cdot 296 \div 4$

1

(d) $\frac{3}{4}$ of 480 g

2

[Turn over

Marks | KU | RI

2.

A student pays a train fare of £24.

If this represents 60% of the full adult fare, what is the full adult fare?

3

3. Brian checks the five day weather forecast for Paris.

| PARIS – FORECAST for 15 January | | |
Maximum (°C)	Minimum (°C)	
Saturday	3	−3	Cloudy
Sunday	2	0	Sunny
Monday	7	4	Cloudy
Tuesday	7	2	Sunny
Wednesday	5	−2	Sunny

Calculate the **mean** minimum temperature for the five day weather forecast.

3

Marks | KU | RE

4.   (*a*)   Write the number $1\cdot5 \times 10^{-1}$ in full.

1

(*b*)   Mark the position of this number on the number line below.

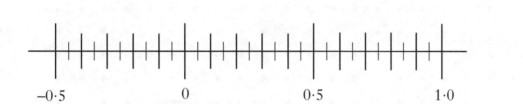

−0·5   0   0·5   1·0

1

[Turn over

DO NOT
WRITE IN
THIS
MARGIN

Marks | KU | R

5. A seaside promenade is to be covered with tiles.

All the tiles are shaped like this.

Here is part of the design of tiles.

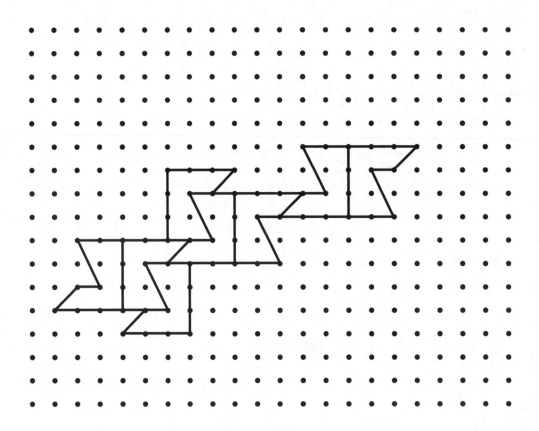

Draw six more tiles to continue the design.   3

DO NOT
WRITE IN
THIS
MARGIN

Marks | KU | RE

6. Two trains run from Aberdeen to London Kings Cross.

They both have **the same journey time.**

	Train 1	Train 2
Aberdeen *Depart*	1455	2125
Kings Cross *Arrive*	2229	

Find the arrival time for Train 2 at Kings Cross.

3

[Turn over

Marks　KU　RI

7. (*a*) Plot the points A (4,6) and C (4,–2) on this grid.

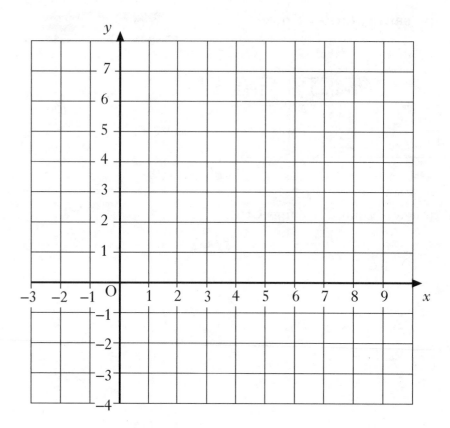

1

(*b*) ABCD is a rhombus with area 24 square units.

Plot B and D on the grid.

3

Marks   KU   RE

8.

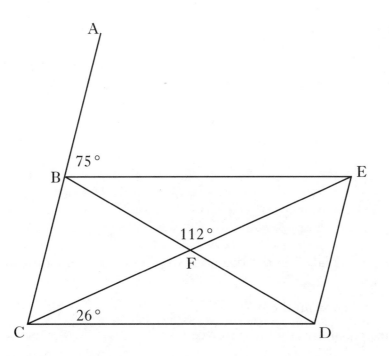

BCDE is a parallelogram.

Angle ABE = 75°, angle ECD = 26°, angle BFE = 112°.

Calculate the size of the angle CBD.

3

[Turn over

Marks

9. There are 1 blue, 2 red and 3 yellow counters in a bag.

(a) A counter is taken from the bag.

What is the probability that the counter is red?

1

(b) The counter is replaced in the bag and two green counters are added to the bag.

A counter is taken from the bag.

What is the probability that it is **not** yellow?

2

DO NOT
WRITE IN
THIS
MARGIN

Marks | KU | RE

10. At Dunure Tennis and Golf Club, the ratio of tennis players to golfers is 100:350.

(a) Express this ratio in its simplest form.

1

(b) The club has been given £16 200.

This money will be divided between the tennis section and the golf section in the same ratio as above.

How much money will be allocated to the tennis section?

3

[END OF QUESTION PAPER]

ADDITIONAL SPACE FOR ANSWERS

FOR OFFICIAL USE

G

	KU	RE
Total marks		

2500/404

NATIONAL
QUALIFICATIONS
2001

WEDNESDAY, 16 MAY
11.35 AM – 12.30 PM

MATHEMATICS
STANDARD GRADE
General Level
Paper 2

Fill in these boxes and read what is printed below.

Full name of centre

Town

Forename(s)

Surname

Date of birth
Day Month Year

Scottish candidate number

Number of seat

1 **You may use a calculator.**

2 Answer as many questions as you can.

3 Write your working and answers in the spaces provided. Additional space is provided at the end of this question-answer book for use if required. If you use this space, write clearly the number of the question involved.

4 Full credit will be given only where the solution contains appropriate working.

5 Before leaving the examination room you must give this book to the invigilator. If you do not you may lose all the marks for this paper.

SCOTTISH
QUALIFICATIONS
AUTHORITY
©

FORMULAE LIST

Circumference of a circle: $C = \pi d$
Area of a circle: $A = \pi r^2$
Curved surface area of a cylinder: $A = 2\pi rh$
Volume of a cylinder: $V = \pi r^2 h$
Volume of a triangular prism: $V = Ah$

Theorem of Pythagoras:

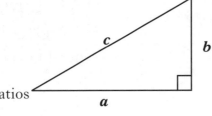

$$a^2 + b^2 = c^2$$

Trigonometric ratios
in a right angled
triangle:

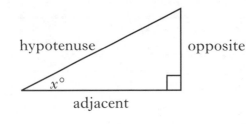

$$\tan x° = \frac{\text{opposite}}{\text{adjacent}}$$

$$\sin x° = \frac{\text{opposite}}{\text{hypotenuse}}$$

$$\cos x° = \frac{\text{adjacent}}{\text{hypotenuse}}$$

Gradient:

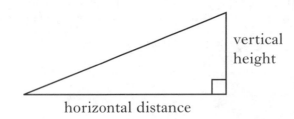

$$\text{Gradient} = \frac{\text{vertical height}}{\text{horizontal distance}}$$

Marks

1. Jayne is 14 years of age and a member of Kelly's Health Club.

   She receives details of next year's subscription rates.

   They are as follows:

Category of member	Payment in full	Payment by instalments
Adult	£390	12 payments of £36
Junior (under 16 years of age)	£195	12 payments of £18
Husband and Wife	£695	12 payments of £65

   (a) Jayne decides to pay by instalments.

   How much extra will she pay?

   2

   (b) Express this extra cost as a percentage of the payment in full.

   Give your answer correct to 1 decimal place.

   3

Marks | KU | RI

2. The number of passengers travelling by bus from Glasgow to Edinburgh was recorded for 20 journeys.

29	45	36	27	41	38	14
48	31	39	24	17	23	34
29	38	42	12	32	36	

(a) Display the information in an ordered stem and leaf diagram.

3

(b) Find the median number of passengers.

1

Marks | KU | RE

3. Shona is planning to buy a new mobile phone.

She knows that she makes between 60 and 120 minutes of calls each month.

Her local phone shop advises that the "All-Talk" or "Talk-Time" tariff are best for her.

They give her the graph below to help her decide.

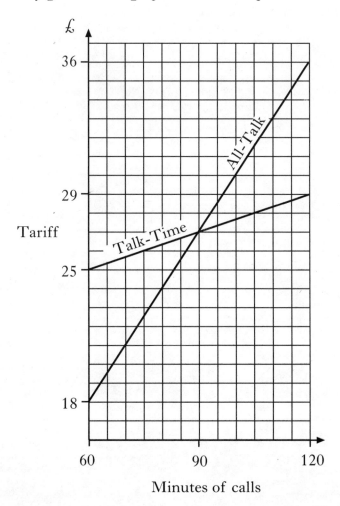

Shona chooses the All-Talk tariff.

Comment on her choice.

2

[Turn over

Marks | KU | R

4. A manufacturer has changed its washing powder so that less powder will be needed for each wash.

As a result the new 1·5 kilogram box gives the same number of washes as the old 2 kilogram box.

A family wash used 96 grams of powder from the old 2 kilogram box.

How much powder will be used for a family wash now?

4

Marks | KU | RE

5. Davina sees this advertisment for CAR HIRE while on holiday in Spain.

UNLIMITED MILEAGE, INSURANCE INCLUDED	
Locus Speedster	3100 pesetas per day
	20 000 pesetas per week
A-Drive Trekcar	5560 pesetas per day
	35 000 pesetas per week
ADD 15% TAX	

She decides to hire the Trekcar for 4 days.

Find the cost, in pounds sterling, of hiring the car if the exchange rate is £1= 256 pesetas.

5

[Turn over

6. Mairi is planning to paint the walls of her room with emulsion paint.

The room is in the shape of a cuboid, with the dimensions shown.

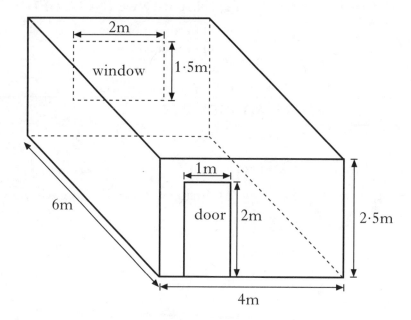

(a) How much paint does Mairi need to paint the walls of her room?

2

(b) Paint is sold only in 1 litre and 2·5 litre tins.

What will be the minimum cost of painting Mairi's room with emulsion?

2

Marks   KU   RE

7. John is laying a concrete floor for his garage.

The floor is to be a rectangle 5·5 metres by 3 metres.

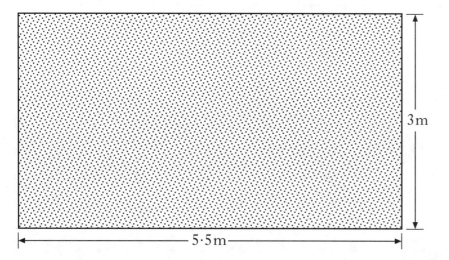

3 m

5·5 m

To check the floor is rectangular, John measures a diagonal.

What should this measurement be?

3

[Turn over

Marks | KU | RI

8. At the Ewington Athletic Club the length of one lap of the track is 400 metres.

In the 10 000 metres race a runner takes an average of 65·2 seconds to complete each lap.

At this pace, will this runner break the race record of 27 minutes 12 seconds?

4

Marks   KU   RE

9. (*a*) Simplify

$$3(2x+4) + 4(x-2).$$

3

(*b*) Solve algebraically the inequality

$$6x + 2 \leq 20.$$

2

[Turn over

Marks | KU | RI

10. The base of a round cake tin has the same area as the base of a square cake tin.

The round cake tin has a radius of 10 centimetres.

 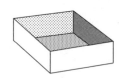

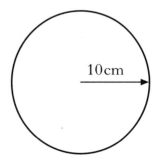 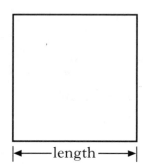

What is the length of the base of the square cake tin?

3

Marks KU RE

11. (*a*) The base of a lift is in the shape of a rectangle with a semi-circular end as shown.

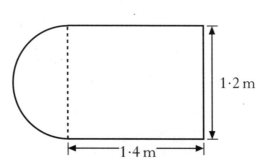

Calculate the area of the base of the lift.

3

(*b*) The lift is in the shape of a prism and is 220 centimetres high.

Find the volume of the lift.

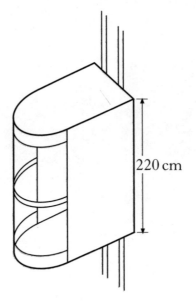

2

[Turn over for Question 12 on *Page fourteen*

Marks   KU   R

12. An architect is designing a room in an attic of a house.

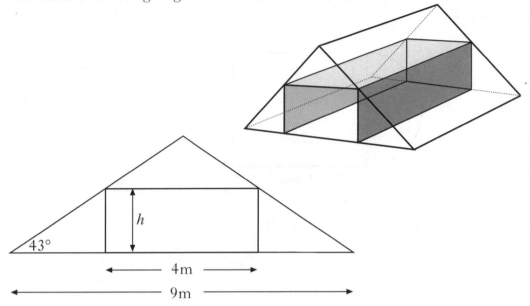

- The room is 4 metres wide.
- The width of the roof is 9 metres.
- The sloping part of the roof makes an angle of 43° with the attic floor.

To satisfy building regulations the height, h, of the room must be **not less than** 2·3 metres.

Does the architect's design satisfy the building regulations?

Give a reason for your answer.

4

[END OF QUESTION PAPER]

FOR OFFICIAL USE

G

KU   RE

Total marks

2500/403

NATIONAL	THURSDAY, 9 MAY	**MATHEMATICS**
QUALIFICATIONS	10.40 AM – 11.15 AM	STANDARD GRADE
2002		General Level
		Paper 1
		Non-calculator

Fill in these boxes and read what is printed below.

Full name of centre

Town

Forename(s)

Surname

Date of birth
Day Month Year   Scottish candidate number   Number of seat

1 **You may not use a calculator.**

2 Answer as many questions as you can.

3 Write your working and answers in the spaces provided. Additional space is provided at the end of this question-answer book for use if required. If you use this space, write clearly the number of the question involved.

4 Full credit will be given only where the solution contains appropriate working.

5 Before leaving the examination room you must give this book to the invigilator. If you do not you may lose all the marks for this paper.

SCOTTISH
QUALIFICATIONS
AUTHORITY

©

FORMULAE LIST

Circumference of a circle:	$C = \pi d$
Area of a circle:	$A = \pi r^2$
Curved surface area of a cylinder:	$A = 2\pi rh$
Volume of a cylinder:	$V = \pi r^2 h$
Volume of a triangular prism:	$V = Ah$

Theorem of Pythagoras:

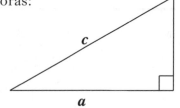

$$a^2 + b^2 = c^2$$

Trigonometric ratios
in a right angled
triangle:

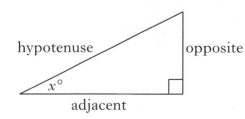

$$\tan x° = \frac{\text{opposite}}{\text{adjacent}}$$

$$\sin x° = \frac{\text{opposite}}{\text{hypotenuse}}$$

$$\cos x° = \frac{\text{adjacent}}{\text{hypotenuse}}$$

Gradient:

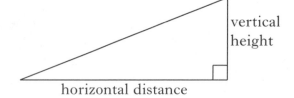

$$\text{Gradient} = \frac{\text{vertical height}}{\text{horizontal distance}}$$

Marks | KU | RE

1. Carry out the following calculations.

(a) $9 \cdot 2 - 3 \cdot 71 + 6 \cdot 47$

1

(b) $7 \cdot 29 \times 8$

1

(c) $687 \div 300$

1

(d) $3 \times 2\frac{3}{4}$

2

[Turn over

DO NOT
WRITE IN
THIS
MARGIN

Marks　KU　RE

2. Davina has a bag of sweets.

It contains three yellow sweets, four purple sweets, two red sweets and six pink sweets.

The corner of her bag is torn and a sweet falls out.

(*a*) What is the probability that this sweet is yellow?

1

(*b*) The sweet that fell out was yellow and she put it in a bin.

What is the probability that the next sweet to fall out is pink?

2

Marks   KU   RE

3. Complete this shape so that it has quarter-turn symmetry about O.

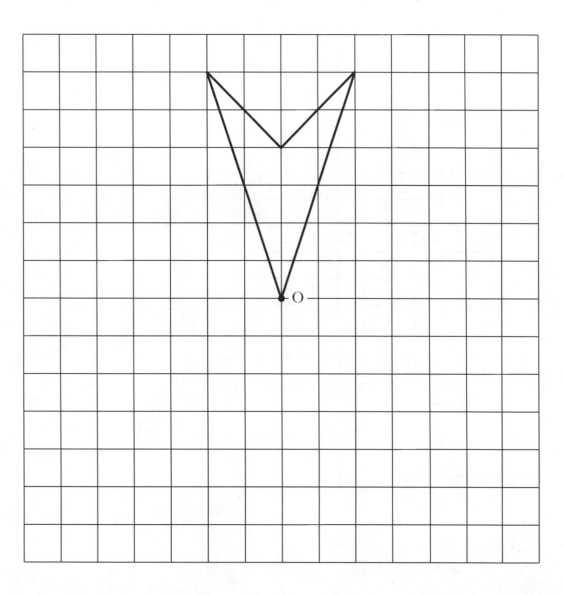

3

4. There are five million people in the United Kingdom aged 15–19.

30% of these five million people regularly watch cartoons.

How many people is this?

2

[Turn over

DO NOT
WRITE IN
THIS
MARGIN

Marks | KU | RE

5. (*a*) On the grid below, plot the points A(–4, –3), B(3, –1) and C(4, 4).

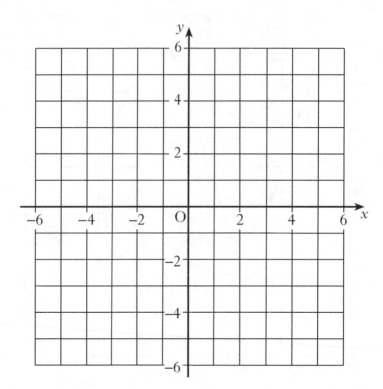

2

(*b*) Find the gradient of the line AB.

2

(*c*) Plot the fourth point D so that shape ABCD is a parallelogram.

Write down the coordinates of point D.

2

Marks KU   RE

6. Starting with the smallest, write the following in order.

$$0{\cdot}404 \qquad \frac{1}{4} \qquad 41\% \qquad 0{\cdot}04 \qquad \frac{4}{10}$$

2

7.

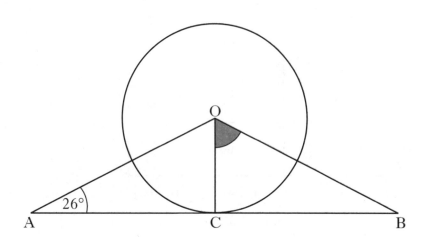

In the above diagram with circle centre O,

- Triangle AOB is isosceles

- AB is a tangent to the circle at C

- Angle CAO is 26°.

Calculate the size of the shaded angle COB.

2

[Turn over

Marks | KU | R

8. The Science and Mathematics marks for 10 students are shown in the table below.

Student	A	B	C	D	E	F	G	H	I	J
Science mark	35	45	65	70	57	25	80	85	10	34
Mathematics mark	41	52	65	75	60	28	84	90	11	37

(a) Using these marks draw a Scattergraph.

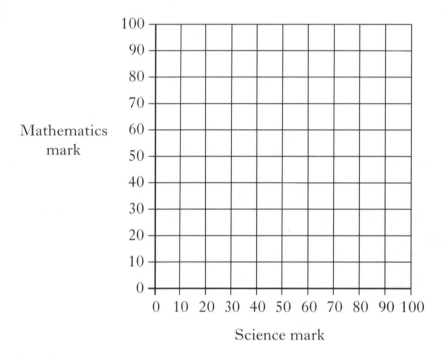

3

(b) Draw a best-fitting line on the graph.   1

(c) A student whose Science mark is 50 was absent from the Mathematics exam.

Using the best-fitting line, estimate this student's Mathematics mark.

1

Marks KU RE

9. A gardener has been measuring the weekly growth rates of plants.

Two of the plants that have been measured are Plant A and Plant B.

One week Plant A is 29 cm high and Plant B is 46 cm high.

The next week Plant A is 57 cm high and Plant B is 71 cm high.

Which plant has grown more in the week and by how much?

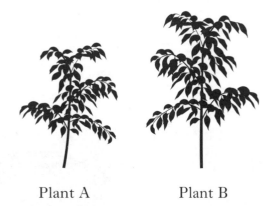

Plant A   Plant B

3

[Turn over for Question 10 on *Page ten*

Marks   KU   RI

10.

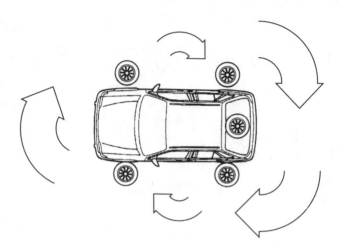

A car has five tyres, one on each of the four road wheels and one on the spare wheel.

Mr Anderson switched his wheels regularly so that all five tyres were used equally.

Last year he travelled 20 000 miles.

How many miles did each tyre do on the road?

3

[END OF QUESTION PAPER]

FOR OFFICIAL USE

G

	KU	RE
Total marks		

2500/404

NATIONAL
QUALIFICATIONS
2002

THURSDAY, 9 MAY
11.35 AM – 12.30 PM

MATHEMATICS
STANDARD GRADE
General Level
Paper 2

Fill in these boxes and read what is printed below.

Full name of centre

Town

Forename(s)

Surname

Date of birth
Day Month Year   Scottish candidate number   Number of seat

1 **You may use a calculator.**

2 Answer as many questions as you can.

3 Write your working and answers in the spaces provided. Additional space is provided at the end of this question-answer book for use if required. If you use this space, write clearly the number of the question involved.

4 Full credit will be given only where the solution contains appropriate working.

5 Before leaving the examination room you must give this book to the invigilator. If you do not you may lose all the marks for this paper.

SCOTTISH
QUALIFICATIONS
AUTHORITY

FORMULAE LIST

Circumference of a circle: $C = \pi d$
Area of a circle: $A = \pi r^2$
Curved surface area of a cylinder: $A = 2\pi rh$
Volume of a cylinder: $V = \pi r^2 h$
Volume of a triangular prism: $V = Ah$

Theorem of Pythagoras:

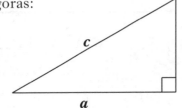

$$a^2 + b^2 = c^2$$

Trigonometric ratios
in a right angled
triangle:

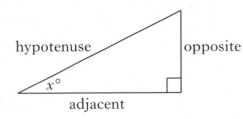

$$\tan x° = \frac{\text{opposite}}{\text{adjacent}}$$

$$\sin x° = \frac{\text{opposite}}{\text{hypotenuse}}$$

$$\cos x° = \frac{\text{adjacent}}{\text{hypotenuse}}$$

Gradient:

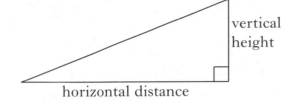

$$\text{Gradient} = \frac{\text{vertical height}}{\text{horizontal distance}}$$

Marks | KU | RE

1. John drives from Edinburgh to Inverness at an average speed of 76 kilometres per hour.

The journey takes him 3 hours 45 minutes.

How far is it from Edinburgh to Inverness?

2

[Turn over

Marks   KU   RE

2. Andrea sees this advertisement for a computer in CompCo.

CompCo
SPECIAL OFFER
£779 + VAT (17·5%)

OUR PROMISE
If you find the same computer at a cheaper price within 1 month, we will **refund double the difference**.

(a) Andrea buys the computer from CompCo.

VAT is 17·5%.

What is the total cost of the computer?

Round your answer to the nearest penny.

3

(b) One week later, Andrea sees the same computer in a different shop at £900 including VAT.

She remembers the promise in the CompCo advertisement and returns to the shop to claim a refund.

How much money should be refunded to her?

2

Marks   KU   RE

3. A column is in the shape of a cylinder.

It is 450 centimetres high and its diameter is 40 centimetres.

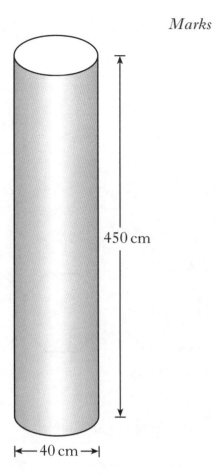

450 cm

|←—40 cm—→|

(a) Find the volume of the column in cubic centimetres.

2

(b) Write your answer to (a) in scientific notation.

1

[Turn over

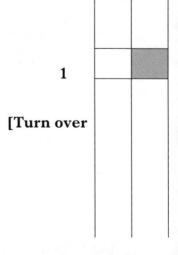

4. A metal fence for a garden is made by joining iron bars as shown below.

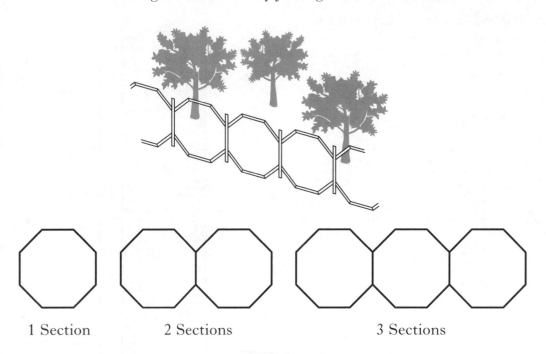

1 Section   2 Sections   3 Sections

(*a*) Complete this table.

Number of sections (*s*)	1	2	3	4		12
Number of iron bars (*b*)	8		22			

2

(*b*) Find a formula for calculating the number of iron bars (*b*), when you know the number of sections (*s*).

2

(*c*) A fence has been made by joining 176 iron bars.

How many sections are in this fence?

2

DO NOT
WRITE IN
THIS
MARGIN

Marks | KU | RE

5. A sum of £1640 is invested in a bank.

The rate of interest is 4·5% per annum.

Calculate the simple interest gained in 9 months.

3

[Turn over

6. PQRS is a rhombus.

Its diagonals PR and SQ are 20 centimetres and 12 centimetres long respectively.

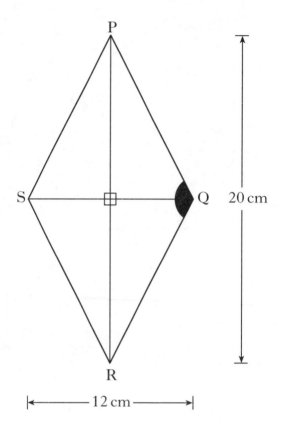

Calculate the size of the shaded angle PQR.

Do not use a scale drawing.

4

Marks KU RE

7. The diagram below shows the wall Jamie has tiled above the bath in his house.

He used rectangular tiles, some of which he halved.

The length of each tile is 30 centimetres.

The breadth of each tile is 20 centimetres.

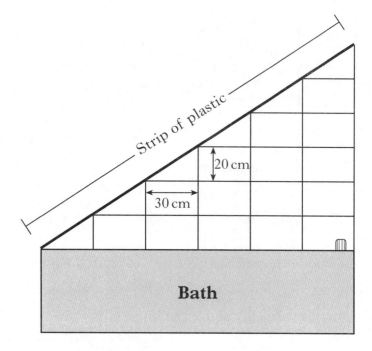

A strip of plastic is fitted along the top of the tiles.

Calculate the length of the strip of plastic.

4

[Turn over

Marks | KU | RI

8.

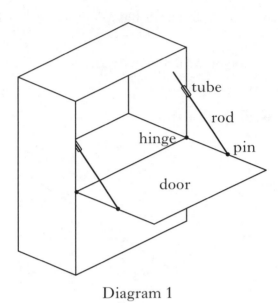

Diagram 1

A cabinet has a door that opens downwards until it is at right angles to the front of the cabinet.

A rod is pinned to the door at point P, 15 centimetres from the hinge, H.

The rod is 35 centimetres long and passes through a tube, at point T.

This tube is 20 centimetres vertically above the hinge.

Marks | KU | RE

8. (continued)

(*a*) Diagram 2 shows the positions of points P, T and H when the door is fully open.

Draw this diagram to a scale of 1:2.

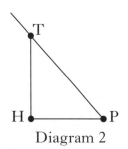

Diagram 2

4

(*b*) Use your scale drawing to find the actual length of the rod between points P and T.

2

[Turn over

Marks | KU | RE

9. (*a*) Solve algebraically the equation

$$4(3x + 2) = 68.$$

3

(*b*) Factorise

$$10y + 15.$$

2

Marks KU RE

10. A joiner is making tables for a new coffee shop.

The shape of the top of a table is a semi-circle as shown below.

AB = 120 centimetres.

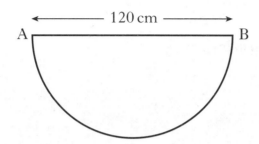

A ←————— 120 cm —————→ B

The top of the table is made of wood and a metal edge is to be fixed to its perimeter.

(*a*) Calculate the total length of the metal edge.

3

(*b*) The coffee shop needs 16 tables.

The joiner has 50 metres of the metal edge in the workshop.

Will this be enough for all sixteen tables?

Give a reason for your answer.

2

[Turn over

Marks | KU | RE

11. The Davidson family is planning to buy a new kitchen using hire purchase.

The cash price of the kitchen is £6300.

The hire purchase price is 22% more than the cash price.

The hire purchase agreement requires a deposit, which is 15% of the cash price, followed by 60 equal instalments.

Calculate the cost of each instalment.

4

[END OF QUESTION PAPER]

ADDITIONAL SPACE FOR ANSWERS

ADDITIONAL SPACE FOR ANSWERS